JR. GRAPHIC MONSTER STORIES

MUMMIES!

MARK CHEATHAM

PowerKiDS
press

New York

Published in 2012 by The Rosen Publishing Group, Inc.
29 East 21st Street, New York, NY 10010

First Edition

Editor: Joanne Randolph
Book Design: Planman Technologies
Illustrations: Planman Technologies

Library of Congress Cataloging-in-Publication Data

Cheatham, Mark.
 Mummies / by Mark Cheatham. — 1st ed.
   p. cm. — (Jr. graphic monster stories)
 Includes index.
 ISBN 978-1-4488-6225-2 (library binding) — ISBN 978-1-4488-6409-6 (pbk.)
 — ISBN 978-1-4488-6410-2 (6-pack)
 1. Mummies—Juvenile literature. I. Title.
 GN293.C54 2012
 393'.3—dc23
                          2011027851

Manufactured in the United States of America
CPSIA Compliance Information: Batch #PLW2102PK: For Further Information contact Rosen
Publishing, New York, New York at 1-800-237-9932

Contents

Main Characters

Howard Carter (1874–1939) English **archaeologist** who discovered the tomb of King Tutankhamen in 1922, one of the greatest discoveries of the twentieth century.

Lord Carnarvon (George Herbert) (1866–1923) Englishman who financed Howard Carter's search for the tomb of King Tutankhamen.

King Tutankhamen (c. 1341–1323 BC) A ruler of ancient Egypt who took the throne when he was 9 years old and died when he was only 19. The discovery of his tomb in 1922 created a worldwide interest in the history of ancient Egypt.

Mummy Facts

- Most scientists think that King Tutankhamen died due to an accident. His leg was badly broken shortly before his death and may have become **infected**.

- During his **reign**, King Tutankhamen worked to create good relations with other kingdoms and countries. As proof of this, scientists point to the many gifts from other countries found in his tomb.

- Mummies were wrapped in long strips of thin linen cloth. The entire mummy was then wrapped in large sheets of cloth. A priest would read spells out loud as the mummy was being wrapped. Spells and writings were supposed to **protect** the mummy in the **afterlife**.

- The Egyptians performed a special **funeral ceremony** called the Opening of the Mouth. They believed that this ceremony allowed the dead person to breathe, speak, eat, and drink in the afterlife.

Mummies!

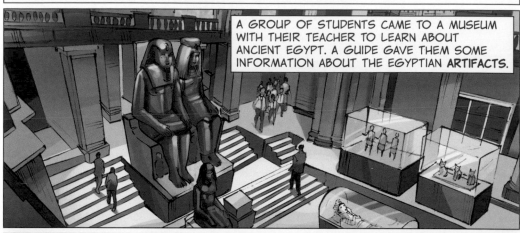

A GROUP OF STUDENTS CAME TO A MUSEUM WITH THEIR TEACHER TO LEARN ABOUT ANCIENT EGYPT. A GUIDE GAVE THEM SOME INFORMATION ABOUT THE EGYPTIAN **ARTIFACTS**.

BODIES OF THE EGYPTIAN DEAD WERE SPECIALLY PREPARED. THEY WERE WRAPPED IN LINEN CLOTH. THIS **PRESERVED** THEM SO THAT THEY COULD LIVE ON IN THE AFTERLIFE.

MUMMIES WERE BURIED IN TOMBS WITH ALL THE THINGS THEY WANTED TO TAKE WITH THEM TO THE NEXT LIFE.

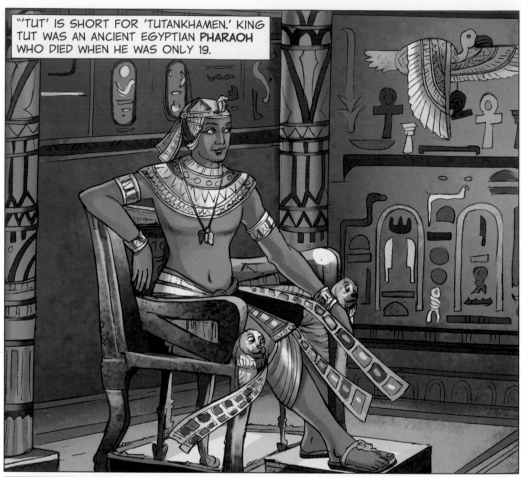

"'TUT' IS SHORT FOR 'TUTANKHAMEN.' KING TUT WAS AN ANCIENT EGYPTIAN **PHARAOH** WHO DIED WHEN HE WAS ONLY 19.

"WHEN EGYPTIAN PHARAOHS DIED, THEY WERE BURIED IN BIG TOMBS WITH MANY TREASURES. ROBBERS OFTEN BROKE INTO THE TOMBS AND STOLE THE TREASURES.

"WHEN ARCHAEOLOGISTS UNCOVERED THESE ROBBED TOMBS CENTURIES LATER, THEY WERE DISAPPOINTED BECAUSE THE TOMBS WERE EMPTY."

THEY EVEN TOOK THE MUMMY!

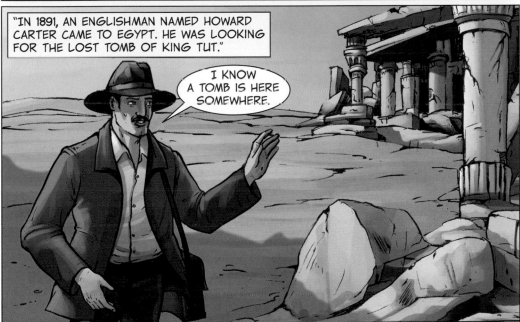

"IN 1891, AN ENGLISHMAN NAMED HOWARD CARTER CAME TO EGYPT. HE WAS LOOKING FOR THE LOST TOMB OF KING TUT."

I KNOW A TOMB IS HERE SOMEWHERE.

"A WEALTHY MAN NAMED LORD CARNARVON GAVE CARTER MONEY TO LOOK FOR TUT'S TOMB. AFTER FIVE YEARS, CARTER STILL HAD NOT FOUND IT. CARNARVON TOLD CARTER TO RETURN TO ENGLAND."

I THINK IT IS TIME TO END THIS SEARCH. I AM RUNNING OUT OF MONEY.

JUST GIVE ME ONE MORE SEASON OF DIGGING. I KNOW I AM CLOSE.

OKAY, BUT JUST ONE MORE SEASON.

"CARTER WENT BACK TO EGYPT. HE TOOK A YELLOW CANARY WITH HIM."

THIS CANARY'S SONG WILL CHEER UP MY HOUSE.

THE GOLDEN BIRD WILL GIVE US LUCK IN FINDING THE TOMB.

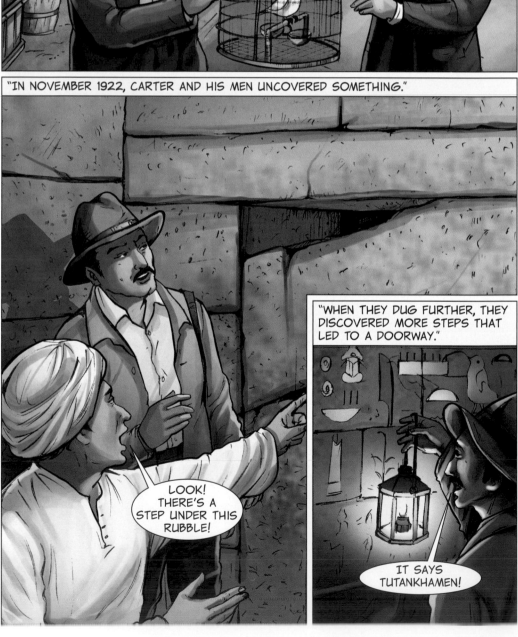

"IN NOVEMBER 1922, CARTER AND HIS MEN UNCOVERED SOMETHING."

LOOK! THERE'S A STEP UNDER THIS RUBBLE!

"WHEN THEY DUG FURTHER, THEY DISCOVERED MORE STEPS THAT LED TO A DOORWAY."

IT SAYS TUTANKHAMEN!

"CARTER SENT A MESSAGE TO LORD CARNARVON IN ENGLAND. HE WOULD WAIT UNTIL LORD CARNARVON ARRIVED BEFORE EXPLORING THE TOMB.

"THREE WEEKS LATER LORD CARNARVON ARRIVED AT THE TOMB."

CAN YOU SEE ANYTHING?

YES, WONDERFUL THINGS!

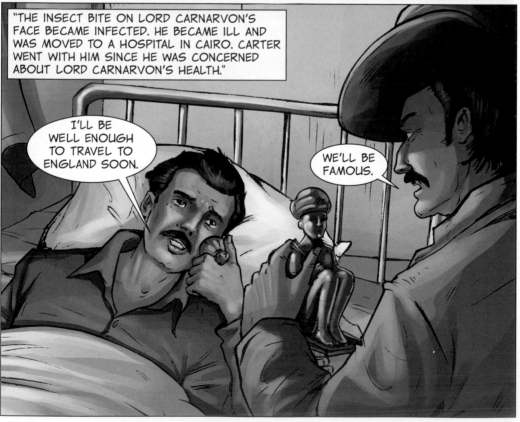

"A STRANGE THING HAPPENED AS CARTER SAT WORKING AT HIS DESK IN CAIRO.

"ALL THE ELECTRIC LIGHTS IN CAIRO SUDDENLY WENT OFF."

THE LIGHTS HAVE GONE OUT ALL OVER THE CITY!

"MEANWHILE ON CARNARVON'S ESTATE IN ENGLAND . . ."

LORD CARNARVON'S DOG STARTED HOWLING, AND THEN SHE SUDDENLY DROPPED DEAD!

WHAT HAS HAPPENED?

"EVEN THE FAMOUS AUTHOR OF THE SHERLOCK HOLMES STORIES SIR ARTHUR CONAN DOYLE, BELIEVED IN KING TUT'S CURSE."

IF SIR ARTHUR BELIEVES IT, IT MUST BE TRUE!

"MORE STORIES SPREAD. SOME PEOPLE GOT SICK AFTER VISITING EGYPTIAN TOMBS."

SHE WAS PERFECTLY HEALTHY THIS MORNING.

"A MAN CLAIMED THAT A LIVE CAT SPRANG OUT OF AN ANCIENT MUMMY CASE.

"PEOPLE EVEN BLAMED A MUMMY FOR THE SINKING OF THE *TITANIC*."

YOU KNOW, THEY SAY THAT A MUMMY'S CURSE SANK THE *TITANIC*. THE MUMMY WAS ON THE SHIP WHEN IT WENT DOWN.

BUT IT SANK *BEFORE* THEY FOUND KING TUT'S TOMB!

WELL, A DIFFERENT MUMMY SANK THE *TITANIC*.

EVEN TODAY THE CURSE OF THE MUMMY TERRIFIES PEOPLE.

RUN! IT'S ALIVE!

AAAHHH!

FORTUNATELY, THE CURSE EXISTS ONLY IN MOVIES AND BOOKS.

OR DOES IT?

More About Mummies

- **The Princess of Amen-Ra** In the 1890s, four Englishmen visited Luxor, on the banks of the Nile River, in Egypt. One of them bought a mummy case from the tomb of the Princess of Amen-Ra. Some think that this mummy case came with a curse. Within a short time, each of the four Englishmen had bad luck. One of the men disappeared in the desert. Another was accidentally shot, a third lost his entire savings, and the fourth man lost his job.

  The mummy case finally made its way to the British Museum, where the night watchman said he heard banging and crying inside the case. Some of the museum workers suffered bad luck. A man died at his desk and the child of another worker died. Within 10 years, about 20 people who came in contact with the case died or suffered bad luck. An archaeologist in New York then purchased the case in 1912. It was carried across the Atlantic Ocean on the ship *Titanic* that sank with a loss of some 1,500 lives.

- **Egyptian Souls** Ancient Egyptians believed that there were five parts to the soul. These were called the ka, ba, akh, sheut, and ren. Egyptians created mummies in order to keep the soul alive after death.

- **Animal Mummies** Ancient Egyptians worshipped animals. Because of this, they made mummies of many different animals such as dogs, cats, cows, crocodiles, and birds. Cat mummies were among the most popular.

Glossary

afterlife (AF-ter-lyf) Where people believe they will go after they die.

archaeologist (ahr-kee-AH-luh-jist) Someone who studies the remains of peoples from the past to understand how they lived.

artifacts (AR-tih-fakts) Objects made by people.

burial chamber (BER-ee-ul CHAYM-bur) A room where bodies are buried.

coffin (KAH-fun) A box that holds a dead body.

curse (KURS) An evil prayer intended to bring misfortune to another.

funeral ceremony (FYOON-rul SER-uh-moh-nee) The service held when burying the dead.

infected (in-FEK-ted) Became sick from germs.

mold spores (MOHLD SPAWRZ) Very small living things that are in the air and can make you sick if you breathe them in.

microbes (MY-krohbz) Very tiny living things that may cause illness.

pharaoh (FER-oh) An ancient Egyptian ruler.

preserved (prih-ZURVD) To have kept something from being lost or from going bad.

protect (pruh-TEKT) To keep from harm.

reign (RAYN) The period of a time that a king or queen rules a country.

revenge (rih-VENJ) Hurting someone in return for hurting you.

sarcophagus (sar-KAH-fuh-gus) A small building of carved stone made to be a grave.

Index

Web Sites

Due to the changing nature of Internet links, PowerKids Press has developed an online list of Web sites related to the subject of this book. This site is updated regularly. Please use this link to access the list:

www.powerkidslinks.com/mons/mummies/